"Down the woody wood path

they set off with a whirl

to go prance and to dance

with the musical girl...."

For Olivia

Happy Birthday from Uncle Darren

With acknowledgement and thanks to the following people, without whose unfailing support, friendship and encouragement along the way all of this would not have been possible;

Joe & Jerry, Kymin, Kevin & Georgie, Kev & Denise, Big Gray and of course Wink & Olivia. Finally, a big thank you to the incredibly talented Carmen Stacey, for bringing Olivia to life

ISBN: 978-0-9954736-0-7

Printed in Suffolk by Gipping Press Ltd

Olivia and the Foxy Foxes

Darren Richardson   Carmen Stacey

Published by Darren George Publishing Ltd.

One frosty and frozen February morn

The kind when grown men wished they'd never been born

The night sky jet black as the clock chimed out two

Not that we'd hear it, not me and not you

For we'd be cuddled and snuggled and snug

Snug as bug in a snuggled up rug

The mums in their nightgowns had long finished their day

The dads in pyjamas were snoring away

The birds had stopped singing, no notes left in their bills

And the buildings stood silent, empty and still

But down in the woods where the bushy things grow

A bushy brown bushy thing started to show

First came a head with a pointy white nose

Then came a leg with some pointy brown toes

Two beady black eyes looked this way and that

And that way and this, looked forward and back

Looked up and looked down and around and around

Peered out in the night without making a sound

Then all at once with a spring and a whoosh

A bushy brown bushy thing sprung out from the bush

It bounced and it pounced and it flounced in the air

That bushy brown tail made of bushy brown hair

All of a sudden it wasn't just one

But two and then three where the one had begun

Then four little bushes sprung into the air

Bushy brown bushes made of bushy brown hair

They rolled and they curled and they stretched and unfurled

Those bushy brown foxes; those bushy brown girls

"Mummy," asked one, "How long will it take

To go down and splash and to splosh in the lake?"

"Mummy," cried two, "It would be ever so good

To roll in the mossy green moss in the wood."

Then "Mummy," sang three as they swirled and they twirled

"Let's go down and dance with the musical girl!

"Now, now," said their mummy standing ever so tall
"Before sploshing or rolling or dancing at all
You must smarten your coats and then tidy your face
And clean and then preen your tails into place"

So the little brown foxes, they licked and they cleaned
Brushed up their coats; had their bushy tails preened
Then bouncing and flouncing and prancing once more
They begged, "Can we dance like we have done before?"
So down the woody wood path they set off with a twirl
To go prance and to dance with the musical girl

Now down through the wood, through the field and the green

Was a place where the bright yellow lights could be seen,

Was the road where the cars went whizzing so fast

So the foxy girls waited until the danger had passed

Then over they crossed while the coast was all clear

With their eyes looking beady and with pricky up ears

And the tall rows of houses stood silent and red

With the people inside them all snuggled in bed

Now I say they were snuggled with eyes all shut tight

But one little girl was up half of the night

Peering into the dark and the garden outside

Her mind was so sleepy but her eyes open wide

She made not a sound as she stood on the floor

Hoping the foxes would come and they'd dance like before

Down past the shed where the pond had a bridge

She'd left bowls of milk from out of the fridge

Apricot pastries that made her tongue lick her lips

And a handful of muffins with milk chocolate chips

Oh what a feast those young foxes would get

But it was now half past two and no sign of them yet

Just as she yawned and turned back to her bed

A brown bushy movement made her turn back her head

And there by the little red flowers and tree

She was sure that a pointy white nose she could see

Yes there it was, a pointy white nose

Two beady black eyes and some pointy brown toes

She crept from her post not a moment too soon

Out through the door marked Olivia's Room

She counted the stairs as she slowly slipped down
And tied tight the belt on her pink dressing gown
By the time that Olivia had opened the door
The foxes were dining, not one but all four

One full of muffin let out a small burp
And the rest at the milk dish were having a slurp
She closed the back door with a soft sneaky squeak
The foxy girls stopped and turned round for a peek

Their long noses twitched and their ears tweaked around

And they stood there dead still not making a sound

Olivia crept down past the green gooseberry bush

Put her finger to her lips and let out a low "shhhhh"

At this point most foxes would surely take flight

Turn on their heels and run off into the night

But these four foxy foxes were out for a dance

No way were they leaving, not even a chance

And Olivia was here for a twirl in the dark

With those golden brown dancers who'd crept through the park

So with a careful approach and a cautious condition

The five foxy dancers took up their silent positions

And as Olivia pressed play on her music machine

All five of them twirled in their musical dream

They danced round the garden in a magical state

All through the flowerbeds and up to the gate

The bushy brown bushes were swirling the air

And Olivia was spinning her own bushy brown hair

All round the garden they swirled and they twirled

They danced and they pranced in their musical world

While the houses around them were silent with sleep

There in the garden they danced off their feet

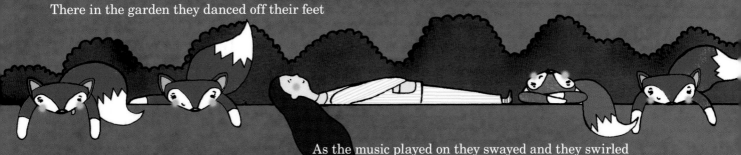

As the music played on they swayed and they swirled

Until they huffed and they puffed; those bushy tailed girls

They waltzed and they tangoed and then waltzed round some more

Until Olivia was bushed and collapsed on the floor

Four bushy brown bushy tails lay by her side
Though worn out and weary, their eyes open wide
As a magical mist fell over the place
They cuddled and snuggled and licked Olivia's face

Yawning and stretching before yawning once more
Olivia waved them goodbye as she trudged to the door
The four bushy brown foxes barked a quiet goodnight
Then slipped out through the bush and were soon out of sight

But Olivia saw nothing as she counted the stairs
Closed the squeaky door tight before saying her prayers
She slipped under the duvet, left her slippers on the rug
And was soon snuggled up like a snuggly snug bug

As soon as her head touched the pillow she fell
Fell deep into a dream where she knew very well
That she would be twirling and whirling once more
And swirling along with the bushy tailed four

In the morning her daddy peered in to see
Olivia snuggled and content as can be
But when he got to the kitchen he was really quite shocked
To find muffins all missing and the door was unlocked

There was no milk for cornflakes or to put in his tea
Just who on earth could the milky thief be?
The apricot pastries, just where did they go?
But you and I know things that grown ups don't know

We know of the muffins eaten all ounce by ounce

And the bushy brown dancers who would bounce and would flounce

Of Olivia's friends who were long out of sight

And the magical things that can happen at night

So when we're asleep and the world is quite dark

There may be some foxy girls out in the park

Being sneaky and sneaking out for the chance

Of a mouth full of muffin and a night full of dance.

If you have enjoyed Olivia and the Foxy Foxes
watch out for a new adventure:

Leo and the Friendly Beaver

coming soon

Find Olivia at www.oliviaandthefoxyfoxes.co.uk

Find out all about us at www.darrengeorgepublishing.com

See what design is all about at www.carmenstacey.com